THE LEFTY GUITARIST'S SURVIVAL HANDBOOK

POCKET GUIDE TO LEFT HANDED GUITAR CHORDS AND SCALES

NEIL D. SANTOS • SCALETRAINER.COM

Copyright © 2013 by Neil D. Santos

Notice of Rights

Printed in the United States of America

First Edition, 2013
Find us online at www.scaletrainer.com
To report errors, please send a note to support@scaletrainer.com

D0594707

For the Southpaws. Guitar is hard enough,
you shouldn't have to learn it using resources
that are upside down and backwards.

When standing up and playing make sure to keep your back straight and have the headstock slightly higher than the body of the guitar. When adjusting the strap keep the strings at a comfortable height for strumming.

When sitting down and playing, place the body of the guitar on your right leg (popular method) or your left leg (classical method). Remember to keep your shoulders loose and don't slouch over the guitar too much or you will develop back problems.

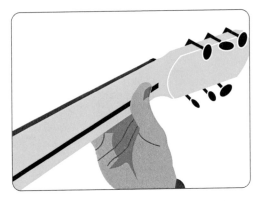

The proper placement of your fretting hand requires your thumb to be directly in the middle of the back of the neck. This type of grip allows your fingers more freedom to move when playing.

Hold your pick as shown to start. Everybody has slightly different ways to hold their picks. When strumming try holding the pick loosely, and when picking hold it a bit tighter.

1

Tuning the Guitar

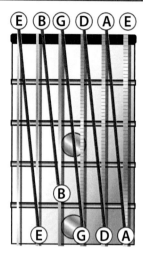

When tuning a guitar by ear simply adjust the of sound of any open string to match the note on the fifth fret on the string above. There is an exception when tuning the B string, you would use the fourth fret.

It is essential that your guitar is in tune in order for all the strings to interact the way that they should. Tuning can be done by ear or by using an electronic tuner. There are many ways to tune the 6 string guitar but the standard method (EADGBE) is designed to make playing chords and scales easier. To help remember the notes of this tuning use the saying:

Every Angry Dog Growls Before Eating

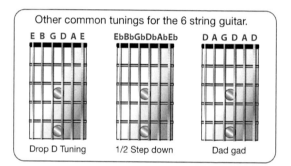

Other common tunings for the 6 string guitar.

| E B G D A E | EbBbGbDbAbEb | D A G D A D |
| Drop D Tuning | 1/2 Step down | Dad gad |

Guitar Tablature

Tablature or **Tab** is a way of notating music for stringed instruments that dates back to the 13th century. A group of horizontal lines create a staff which represent each of the instrument's strings. The top line represents the highest pitched string on the instrument. Numbers are placed on the lines indicating which fret number should be pressed down and played. A zero placed on the string indicates that an open note should be played. Tablature is read from left to right similar to a sentence.

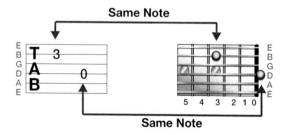

A note written in TAB and where it would appear on the neck.

Reading Chord Grids

Reading chord grids is super easy. The first thing you need to realize is that you're only looking at a small portion of the neck. The section being illustrated is indicated by fret numbers running alongside.

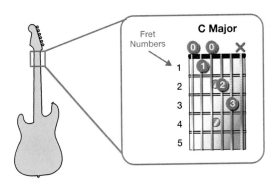

The Anatomy of a Chord Grid

✗ = This string should be muted with your fretting hand

⓪ = This string should is played without a finger on it and is considered open

② = This string should is played where it appears with the finger indicated

⌣ = The notes connected by this line are all held using one finger

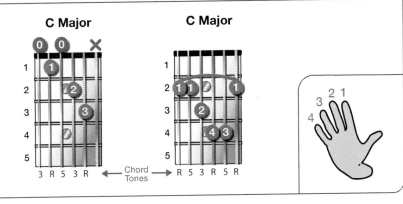

Reading Scale Grids

Scale grids share a lot of their same traits with chord grids. However, scale grids are displayed horizontally rather than vertically. They are also displayed upside down with the thickest string closest to the reader. This mimics the appearance of the neck when holding the guitar with the thickest string (low E) being closest to the eyes.

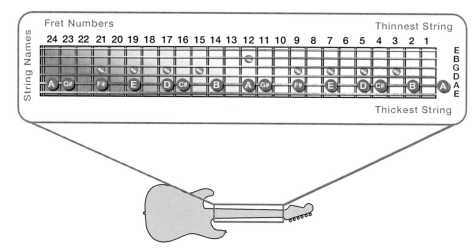

The Anatomy of a Scale Grid

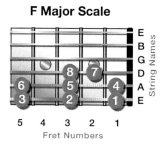

F Major Scale

Fret Numbers

A scale grid shows all the possible notes in a scale but they are not meant to be played all at the same time. Typically scales are utilized one or two notes at a time to create melodies. For example, in order to play the scale illustrated from the lowest to highest note you would play them in the order indicated by the orange circles. However, you could play these notes in any order.

Finding the Notes on the Neck

There are two approaches to learning all the notes on the neck. The first way is to simply drill them into your head one at a time. I've tried this on several occasions without much luck. The most that I could ever remember successfully were the notes on the top two strings. That is when I realized the second method to learning all the notes which isn't about memorizing every note on the neck, it's about finding them quickly. Using octave shapes and the notes on the top two strings I could easily find and name any note on the neck in a matter of seconds.

Step 1: Memorize the notes on the top two strings starting with the notes on the 3, 5, 7, 9, and 12th frets. These have fret markers and are mostly natural notes without sharps or flats.

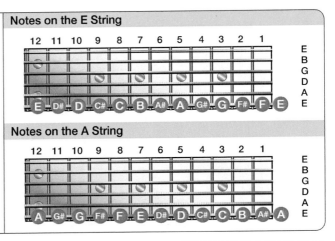

Step 2: Use these octave fingerings to find different locations of any note.

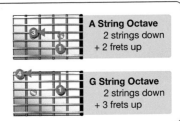

Find a Higher Note

Step 3: Find a higher version of any note starting from a low version you know and follow it upwards.

Identify a Higher Note

Step 3: identify any higher note by moving it downwards to a low version on the top strings that you know.

Open Chords

Open Chords are played within the first few frets on the guitar and include notes on strings that are not fretted and thus considered to be "open" strings. Open chords are also referred to as Cowboy Chords and have a fuller and more robust sound then barre chords.

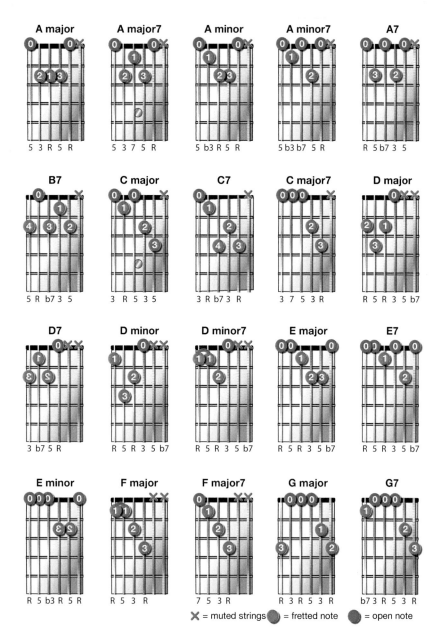

A major	A major7	A minor	A minor7	A7
5 3 R 5 R	5 3 7 5 R	5 b3 R 5 R	5 b3 b7 5 R	R 5 b7 3 5

B7	C major	C7	C major7	D major
5 R b7 3 5	3 R 5 3 5	3 R b7 3 R	3 7 5 3 R	R 5 R 3 5 b7

D7	D minor	D minor7	E major	E7
3 b7 5 R	R 5 R 3 5 b7	R 5 R 3 5 b7	R 5 R 3 5 b7	R 5 R 3 5 b7

E minor	F major	F major7	G major	G7
R 5 b3 R 5 R	R 5 3 R	7 5 3 R	R 3 R 5 3 R	b7 3 R 5 3 R

✗ = muted strings   ◗ = fretted note   ● = open note

6

Power Chords

Power chords are not really chords, because they contain no third degree to distinguish them as major or minor. They are made up of only two notes, a root note and it's fifth interval. When played through a distorted amp however these two notes sound huge. The simple interval of a fifth reacts well to the distorted signal where a regular chord would sound muddy and incoherent. Power chords are easy to play and lend themselves to fast chord changes and riffs.

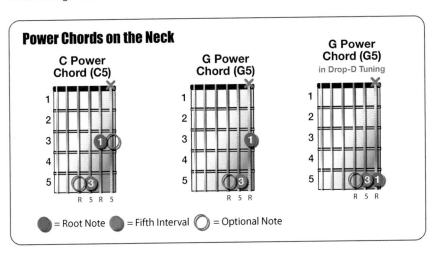

Power Chords on the Neck

C Power Chord (C5)

G Power Chord (G5)

G Power Chord (G5)
in Drop-D Tuning

● = Root Note ● = Fifth Interval ◯ = Optional Note

Because power chords have no thirds in them it can be hard to know which key they belong to. The answer lies in their root motion from chord to chord. Typically all the root notes in a song will outline a specific scale which can help to identify the song's key.

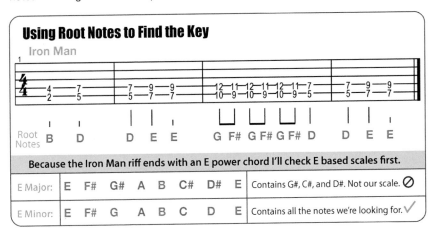

Using Root Notes to Find the Key

Iron Man

Because the Iron Man riff ends with an E power chord I'll check E based scales first.

E Major:	E	F#	G#	A	B	C#	D#	E	Contains G#, C#, and D#. Not our scale. ⊘
E Minor:	E	F#	G	A	B	C	D	E	Contains all the notes we're looking for. ✓

Barre Chords

If open chords were all we had to compose with life would get pretty boring. Even with the use of a capo we would be extremely limited in our options. Luckily someone came up with **Barre Chords** to broaden our chord possibilities. A barre chord utilizes the first finger on a player's fretting hand to act as a movable capo that slides along behind the chords shape allowing it to be played anywhere on the neck.

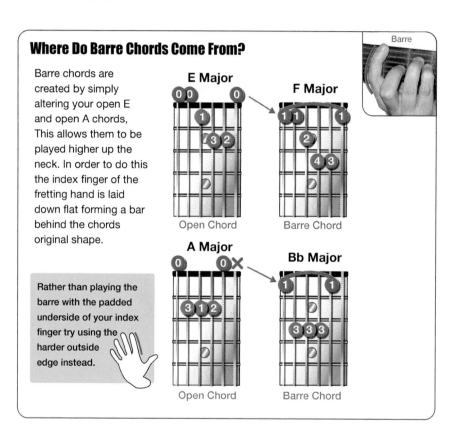

Where Do Barre Chords Come From?

Barre chords are created by simply altering your open E and open A chords, This allows them to be played higher up the neck. In order to do this the index finger of the fretting hand is laid down flat forming a bar behind the chords original shape.

Rather than playing the barre with the padded underside of your index finger try using the harder outside edge instead.

E Major — Open Chord

F Major — Barre Chord

A Major — Open Chord

Bb Major — Barre Chord

Barre

Suspended Chords

A suspended (sus) chord is a chord that has no major or minor third. The third is replaced with either a major second or more commonly a perfect fourth. The absence of a third gives these chords an open and pleasant sound. In the rare instance that a seventh is added it would be a minor seventh. The term suspended comes from classical music where a note from a previous chord would carry over (be suspended) into the next chord. In modern music it simply refers to the harmonic construction of the chord.

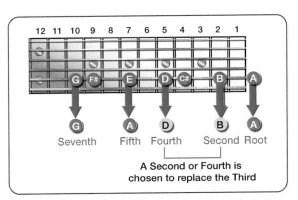

Making a sus chord from an A major scale

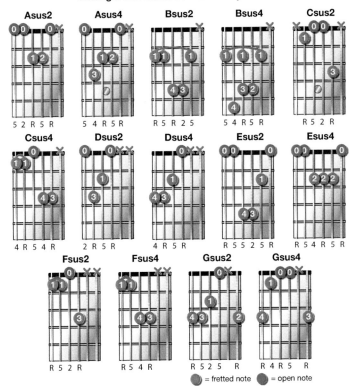

E String Based Chords

All of these chords use the notes of the top "E" string as their root. For example, if you wanted to play a C major chord simply line up the top finger of the major chord shape to the C on the eighth fret.

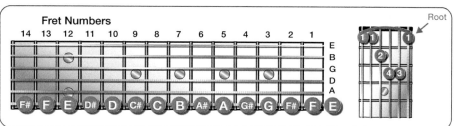

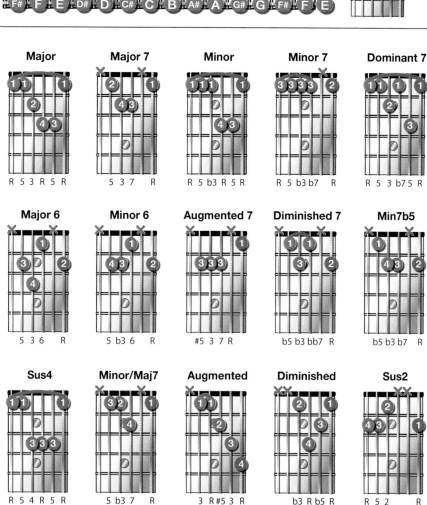

Major	Major 7	Minor	Minor 7	Dominant 7
R 5 3 R 5 R	5 3 7 R	R 5 b3 R 5 R	R 5 b3 b7 R	R 5 3 b7 5 R

Major 6	Minor 6	Augmented 7	Diminished 7	Min7b5
5 3 6 R	5 b3 6 R	#5 3 7 R	b5 b3 bb7 R	b5 b3 b7 R

Sus4	Minor/Maj7	Augmented	Diminished	Sus2
R 5 4 R 5 R	5 b3 7 R	3 R#5 3 R	b3 R b5 R	R 5 2 R

10

All of these chords use the notes on the "A" string as their root. For example, if you wanted to play a C major chord simply line up the top finger of the major chord shape to the C on the third fret.

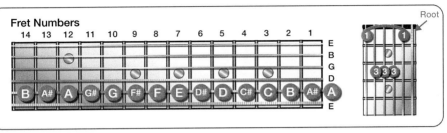

Fret Numbers

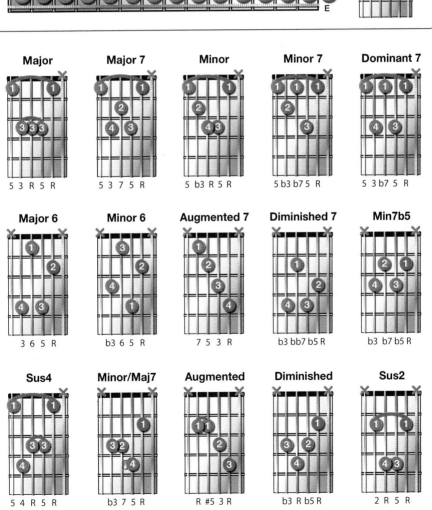

Major	Major 7	Minor	Minor 7	Dominant 7
5 3 R 5 R	5 3 7 5 R	5 b3 R 5 R	5 b3 b7 5 R	5 3 b7 5 R

Major 6	Minor 6	Augmented 7	Diminished 7	Min7b5
3 6 5 R	b3 6 5 R	7 5 3 R	b3 bb7 b5 R	b3 b7 b5 R

Sus4	Minor/Maj7	Augmented	Diminished	Sus2
5 4 R 5 R	b3 7 5 R	R #5 3 R	b3 R b5 R	2 R 5 R

D String Based Chords

All of these chords use the notes on the "D" string as their root. For example, if you wanted to play a C major chord simply line up the top finger of the major chord shape to the C on the tenth fret.

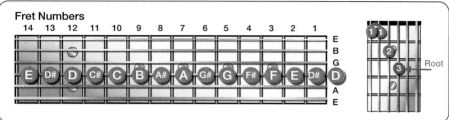

Fret Numbers

| 14 | 13 | 12 | 11 | 10 | 9 | 8 | 7 | 6 | 5 | 4 | 3 | 2 | 1 |

E D# D C# C B A# A G# G F# F E D# D

Root

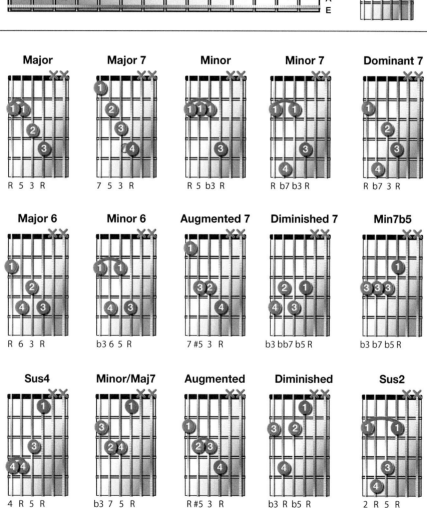

Major	Major 7	Minor	Minor 7	Dominant 7
R 5 3 R	7 5 3 R	R 5 b3 R	R b7 b3 R	R b7 3 R

Major 6	Minor 6	Augmented 7	Diminished 7	Min7b5
R 6 3 R	b3 6 5 R	7 #5 3 R	b3 bb7 b5 R	b3 b7 b5 R

Sus4	Minor/Maj7	Augmented	Diminished	Sus2
4 R 5 R	b3 7 5 R	R #5 3 R	b3 R b5 R	2 R 5 R

12

Major Seventh Arpeggio

The Major Seventh Arpeggio can be thought of as broken major seventh chord meaning the notes of the chord are played separately one after the other rather than strummed all at once.

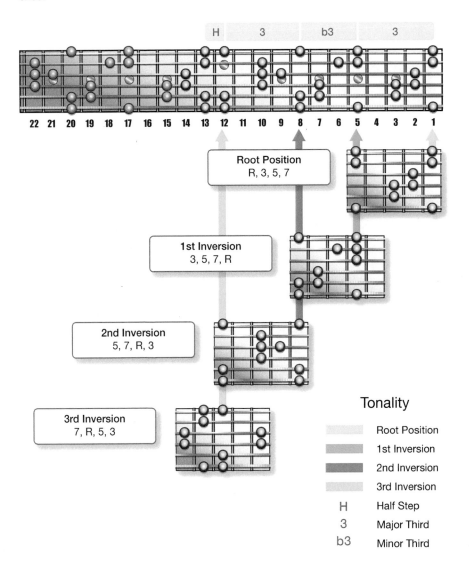

Root Position
R, 3, 5, 7

1st Inversion
3, 5, 7, R

2nd Inversion
5, 7, R, 3

3rd Inversion
7, R, 5, 3

Tonality

	Root Position
	1st Inversion
	2nd Inversion
	3rd Inversion
H	Half Step
3	Major Third
b3	Minor Third

Minor Seventh Arpeggio

The Minor Seventh Arpeggio can be thought of as broken minor seventh chord meaning the notes of the chord are played separately one after the other rather than strummed all at once.

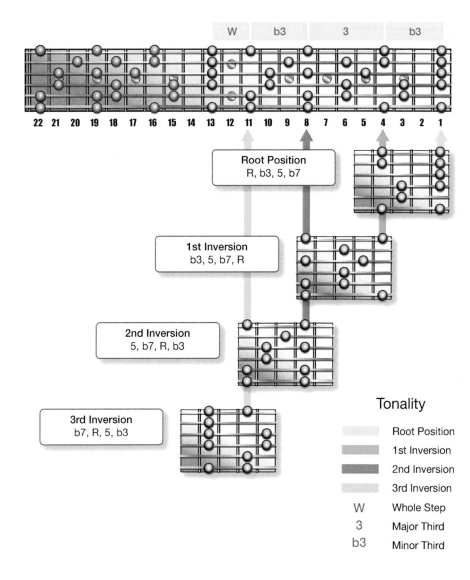

Root Position
R, b3, 5, b7

1st Inversion
b3, 5, b7, R

2nd Inversion
5, b7, R, b3

3rd Inversion
b7, R, 5, b3

Tonality

- Root Position
- 1st Inversion
- 2nd Inversion
- 3rd Inversion
- W — Whole Step
- 3 — Major Third
- b3 — Minor Third

Dominant Seventh Arpeggio

The Dominant Seventh Arpeggio can be thought of as broken dominant seventh chord meaning the notes of the chord are played separately one after the other rather than strummed all at once.

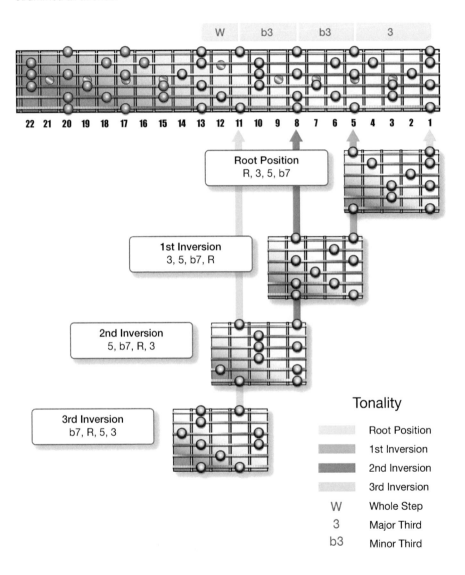

Root Position
R, 3, 5, b7

1st Inversion
3, 5, b7, R

2nd Inversion
5, b7, R, 3

3rd Inversion
b7, R, 5, 3

Tonality

	Root Position
	1st Inversion
	2nd Inversion
	3rd Inversion
W	Whole Step
3	Major Third
b3	Minor Third

Minor Major Seventh Arpeggio

All of these chords use the notes on the "D" string as their root. For example, if you wanted to play a C major chord simply line up the top finger of the major chord shape to the C on the tenth fret.

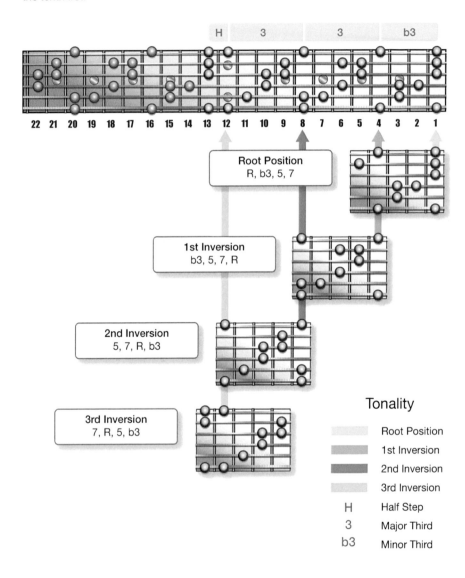

Root Position
R, b3, 5, 7

1st Inversion
b3, 5, 7, R

2nd Inversion
5, 7, R, b3

3rd Inversion
7, R, 5, b3

Tonality

	Root Position
	1st Inversion
	2nd Inversion
	3rd Inversion
H	Half Step
3	Major Third
b3	Minor Third

Minor Seven Flat Five Arpeggio

The Minor Seven Flat Five Arpeggio can be thought of as broken minor seven flat five chord meaning the notes of the chord are played separately one after the other rather than strummed all at once.

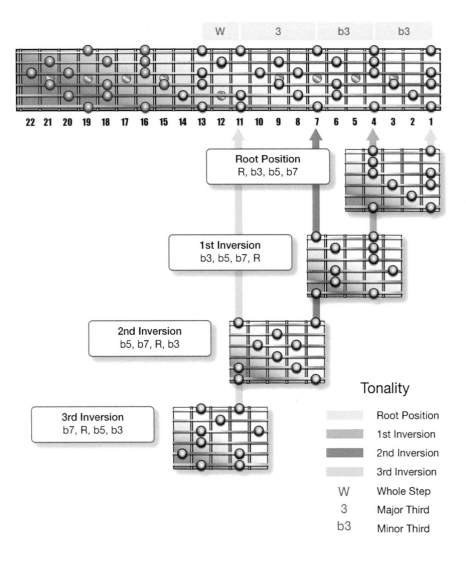

17

Minor & Major Pentatonic

The Minor / Major Pentatonic scale is usually the first scale guitarists learn. The major pentatonic and the minor pentatonic scales each contain the same five notes so they are considered related.

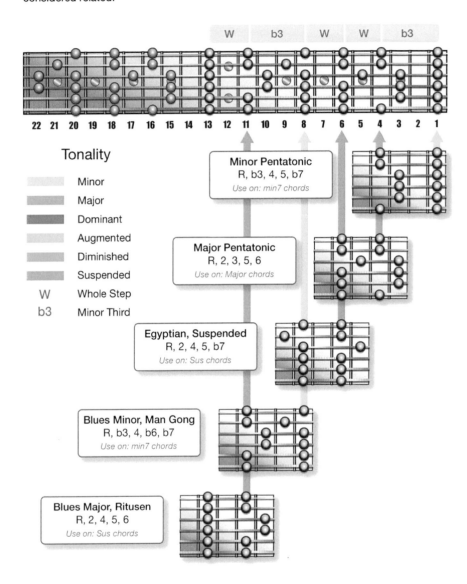

Tonality

Minor
Major
Dominant
Augmented
Diminished
Suspended
W — Whole Step
b3 — Minor Third

Minor Pentatonic
R, b3, 4, 5, b7
Use on: min7 chords

Major Pentatonic
R, 2, 3, 5, 6
Use on: Major chords

Egyptian, Suspended
R, 2, 4, 5, b7
Use on: Sus chords

Blues Minor, Man Gong
R, b3, 4, b6, b7
Use on: min7 chords

Blues Major, Ritusen
R, 2, 4, 5, 6
Use on: Sus chords

The Blues Scale

The Blues scale is basically the minor - major pentatonic scale with an added note. The "blue note" that we add is the #4 and it gives the scale a bit of swagger.

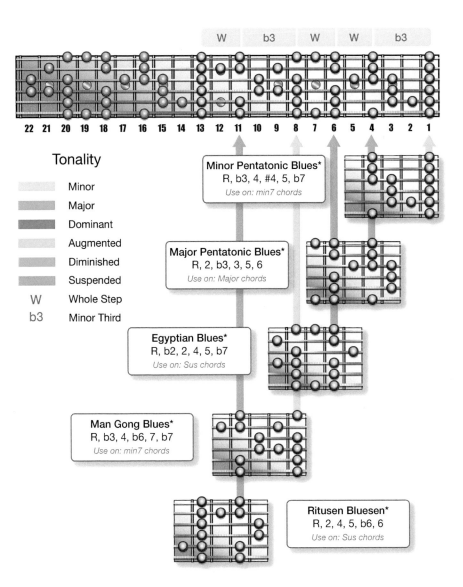

Tonality

- Minor
- Major
- Dominant
- Augmented
- Diminished
- Suspended
- W   Whole Step
- b3   Minor Third

Minor Pentatonic Blues*
R, b3, 4, #4, 5, b7
Use on: min7 chords

Major Pentatonic Blues*
R, 2, b3, 3, 5, 6
Use on: Major chords

Egyptian Blues*
R, b2, 2, 4, 5, b7
Use on: Sus chords

Man Gong Blues*
R, b3, 4, b6, 7, b7
Use on: min7 chords

Ritusen Bluesen*
R, 2, 4, 5, b6, 6
Use on: Sus chords

* *Completely fictitious name*

19

The Major Blues Scale

The Major Blues scale is basically the Minor Blues scale with a different root note. The "blue note" that we add now functions as the b3 and it gives the scale a bit of edge to an overall major sound.

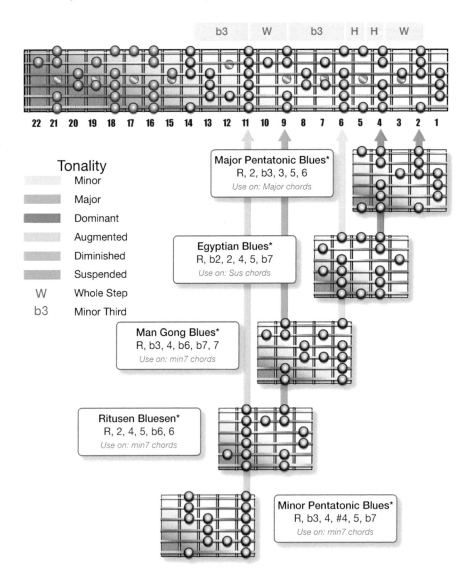

Tonality
- Minor
- Major
- Dominant
- Augmented
- Diminished
- Suspended
- W — Whole Step
- b3 — Minor Third

Major Pentatonic Blues*
R, 2, b3, 3, 5, 6
Use on: Major chords

Egyptian Blues*
R, b2, 2, 4, 5, b7
Use on: Sus chords

Man Gong Blues*
R, b3, 4, b6, b7, 7
Use on: min7 chords

Ritusen Bluesen*
R, 2, 4, 5, b6, 6
Use on: min7 chords

Minor Pentatonic Blues*
R, b3, 4, #4, 5, b7
Use on: min7 chords

* *Completely fictitious name*

Dominant Pentatonic

The Dominant Pentatonic is considered a modal pentatonic scale. It's a simplified version of the Mixolydian mode from from the major scale. It's like the major scale with attitude.

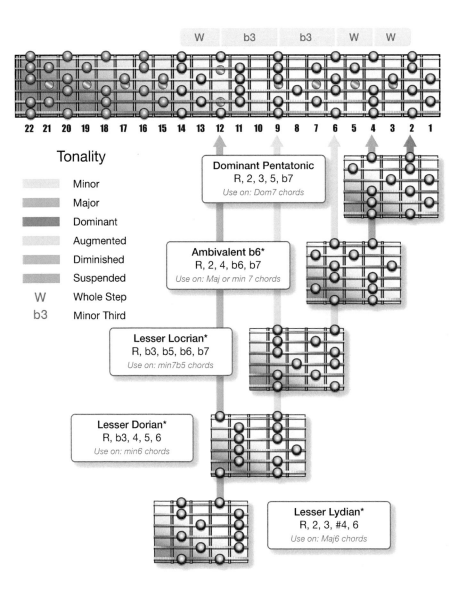

Tonality

- Minor
- Major
- Dominant
- Augmented
- Diminished
- Suspended
- W — Whole Step
- b3 — Minor Third

Dominant Pentatonic
R, 2, 3, 5, b7
Use on: Dom7 chords

Ambivalent b6*
R, 2, 4, b6, b7
Use on: Maj or min 7 chords

Lesser Locrian*
R, b3, b5, b6, b7
Use on: min7b5 chords

Lesser Dorian*
R, b3, 4, 5, 6
Use on: min6 chords

Lesser Lydian*
R, 2, 3, #4, 6
Use on: Maj6 chords

* *Completely fictitious name*

The Melodic Minor Pentatonic is considered a modal pentatonic scale. It's a simplified version of the Melodic Minor scale, a jazzier version of the Minor scale.

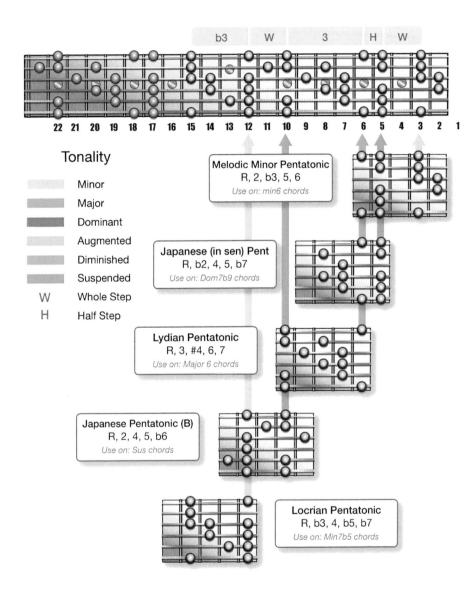

Tonality

Minor
Major
Dominant
Augmented
Diminished
Suspended
W   Whole Step
H   Half Step

Melodic Minor Pentatonic
R, 2, b3, 5, 6
Use on: min6 chords

Japanese (in sen) Pent
R, b2, 4, 5, b7
Use on: Dom7b9 chords

Lydian Pentatonic
R, 3, #4, 6, 7
Use on: Major 6 chords

Japanese Pentatonic (B)
R, 2, 4, 5, b6
Use on: Sus chords

Locrian Pentatonic
R, b3, 4, b5, b7
Use on: Min7b5 chords

The modes of the major scale are very popular in all forms of music. The Aeolian (Natural Minor), and Mixolydian modes as well as the Ionian see a lot of use in rock, folk, pop, classical, and jazz music.

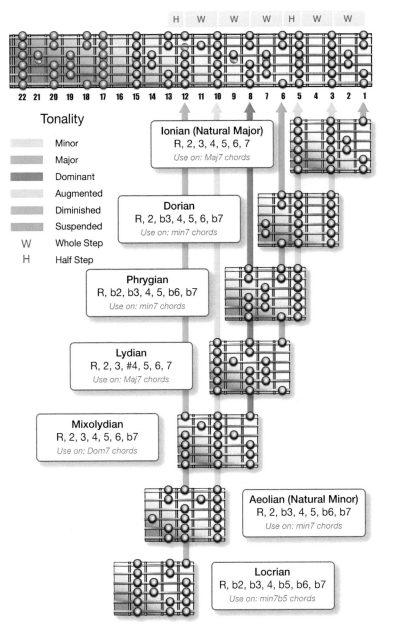

Tonality

- Minor
- Major
- Dominant
- Augmented
- Diminished
- Suspended
- W Whole Step
- H Half Step

Ionian (Natural Major)
R, 2, 3, 4, 5, 6, 7
Use on: Maj7 chords

Dorian
R, 2, b3, 4, 5, 6, b7
Use on: min7 chords

Phrygian
R, b2, b3, 4, 5, b6, b7
Use on: min7 chords

Lydian
R, 2, 3, #4, 5, 6, 7
Use on: Maj7 chords

Mixolydian
R, 2, 3, 4, 5, 6, b7
Use on: Dom7 chords

Aeolian (Natural Minor)
R, 2, b3, 4, 5, b6, b7
Use on: min7 chords

Locrian
R, b2, b3, 4, b5, b6, b7
Use on: min7b5 chords

Melodic Minor

The Melodic Minor scale is good to learn if you're interested in jazz improvisation. The main reason for its appeal is due to its seventh mode, the Altered Dominant scale, a great scale to pair with Altered Dominant Chords.

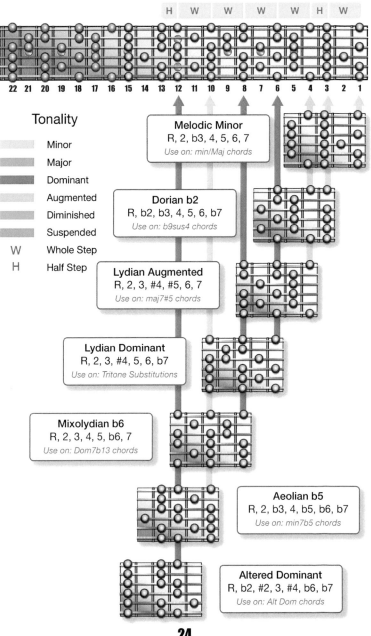

H   W   W   W   W   H   W

22 21 20 19 18 17 16 15 14 13 12 11 10 9 8 7 6 5 4 3 2 1

Tonality

- Minor
- Major
- Dominant
- Augmented
- Diminished
- Suspended
- **W** Whole Step
- **H** Half Step

Melodic Minor
R, 2, b3, 4, 5, 6, 7
Use on: min/Maj chords

Dorian b2
R, b2, b3, 4, 5, 6, b7
Use on: b9sus4 chords

Lydian Augmented
R, 2, 3, #4, #5, 6, 7
Use on: maj7#5 chords

Lydian Dominant
R, 2, 3, #4, 5, 6, b7
Use on: Tritone Substitutions

Mixolydian b6
R, 2, 3, 4, 5, b6, 7
Use on: Dom7b13 chords

Aeolian b5
R, 2, b3, 4, b5, b6, b7
Use on: min7b5 chords

Altered Dominant
R, b2, #2, 3, #4, b6, b7
Use on: Alt Dom chords

24

Harmonic Minor

The Harmonic Minor scale has nearly all the same notes as the natural minor scale except for the seventh degree. This gives it a very classical sound.

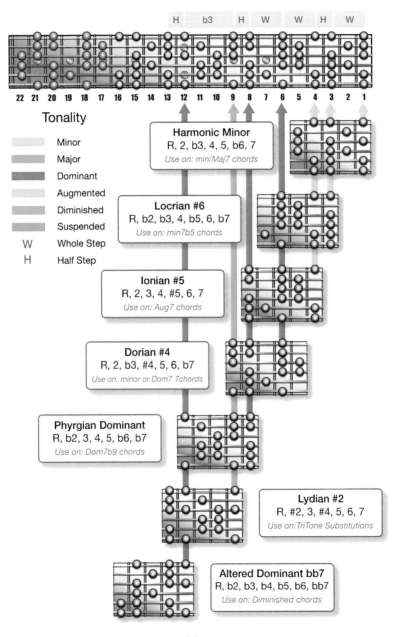

| H | b3 | H | W | | W | H | W |

Tonality

Minor
Major
Dominant
Augmented
Diminished
Suspended
W Whole Step
H Half Step

Harmonic Minor
R, 2, b3, 4, 5, b6, 7
Use on: min/Maj7 chords

Locrian #6
R, b2, b3, 4, b5, 6, b7
Use on: min7b5 chords

Ionian #5
R, 2, 3, 4, #5, 6, 7
Use on: Aug7 chords

Dorian #4
R, 2, b3, #4, 5, 6, b7
Use on: minor or Dom7 7chords

Phyrgian Dominant
R, b2, 3, 4, 5, b6, b7
Use on: Dom7b9 chords

Lydian #2
R, #2, 3, #4, 5, 6, 7
Use on: TriTone Substitutions

Altered Dominant bb7
R, b2, b3, b4, b5, b6, bb7
Use on: Diminished chords

Whole Tone Scale

The Whole Tone scale include six notes that are each a major 2nd or a whole step apart. It is considered a symmetrical scale and its sound does not give the listener a strong sense of a key center or tonality.

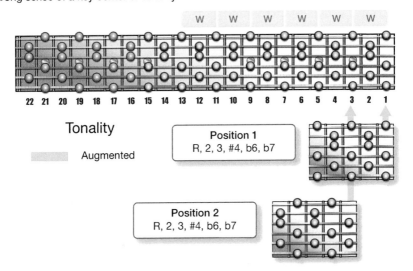

Tonality

Augmented

Position 1
R, 2, 3, #4, b6, b7

Position 2
R, 2, 3, #4, b6, b7

Diminished Scale

The Diminished scale is created from alternating whole step and half step intervals. This formula leaves us with two modes, the whole-half diminished and the half-whole diminished. Both of these scales are considered symmetrical scales.

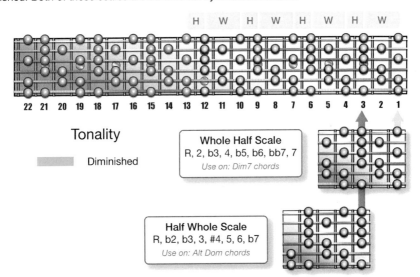

Tonality

Diminished

Whole Half Scale
R, 2, b3, 4, b5, b6, bb7, 7
Use on: Dim7 chords

Half Whole Scale
R, b2, b3, 3, #4, 5, 6, b7
Use on: Alt Dom chords

26

Made in the USA
San Bernardino, CA
13 August 2018